The Hidden I

Te...

Cover Design by Stephen Paul West

Visit the Author at: **www.LosEllis.com**

LIBRARY OF CONGRESS CATALOGING-IN-PUBLICATION DATA

Ellis, Los
The Hidden Keys to Life and Business Success / Los Ellis
p. cm.
• • • •

Summary: The world may appear too complex. Things may seem murky. Finding success may seem difficult. However, the solutions are in the basic keys found in Life and Business. This booklet will show you the easy keys to complex mysteries.

ISBN - 978-1493529032

Best Selling Books Publications

DEDICATION

To all the clients I have worked with over the years. I have learned my craft by helping you achieve your own personal goals, career satisfaction and success.

Endorsements

"Los is a great mentor, with brilliant business acumen and he has the ability to lead leaders. I recommend Los Ellis 100%"

Aldwyn Sappleton, Economist - Oklahoma Dept. of Commerce

• • • •

"Los is a talented professional with the end goal of making our efforts more efficient and effective"

Paul Sengupta Strategy & Planning - Sr. Manager – Hewlett Packard

• • • •

"I was truly impressed with Los' High Energy, talent, leadership, networking capacity and fine observation." Los is a great asset for any company."

Wei Luo -Founder and CEO - China-US Entrepreneurship Academy, LLC

• • • •

"Los is an amazing speaker that will fill the room with energy and motivation."

Tina Fields, Business Systems Analyst – Wells Fargo

• • • •

"I've listened to Los address many different audiences – business leaders, social organizations, college professionals and even high-school students. Each time he delivered a stunning, high-powered presentation that was exactly what the audience needed."

Stephen Paul West – Austin Novelist – Best Selling Book Publications.

• • • •

"With Los on your side you can't go wrong"

Manos Paul – President and CEO - SecuRisk Solutions Inc.

• • • •

ACKNOWLEDGEMENTS

Special thanks for helping me create this book go to:

Delta Sigma Pi, whose standard of excellence has provided me a blueprint to follow and work effectively each day.

All my well-over 100 universities, school districts, municipalities and corporate clients who have used me over the years as a coach in their personal brand development.

My family and close circle of friends who have supported me and provided me a wealth of insight.

And most important, Kendrick, my nephew, whose inspiration encouraged me to go for it, and whose love and support made it possible.

Knowledge to Succeed

Collection 1 - Business Keys

Hidden Keys to Life and Business Success by Los Ellis.

Many people have passed along great hidden (keys) wisdom and advice to me throughout my years of life. When I applied their wisdom and advice to my personal development, I realized these hidden keys were empowering and should be shared with others. Since my name is 'Los' people started to call these hidden keys 'Los-isms'. In a short time, I started receiving letters and testimonials about how my Los-isms inspired them to become better college students, business professionals and everyday hardworking citizens. I decided to write this book to inspire readers to identify the simple, yet strengthening, hidden keys introduced in "Los-isms" to improve their personal life and professional image.

This book is a collection of those Los-isms and these pages create a desk/pocket reference book written to enhance the preparedness of business professionals and individuals looking for an "EXTRA" Ordinary advantage in the world of business and personal development.

What are Los-isms? – Los-isms are experienced ideas and practices used in many businesses, households and organizations. Across the country, businesses, family households and organizations use Los-isms each day to help talented people and those they trust gain a winning start to success.

Who should read The Hidden Keys of Life and Business Success? – You should own and regularly read issues of "The Hidden Keys to Life and Business Success" if you want to advance quickly and exceed the boundaries of your peers and other talented business men and women expectations in your organizations, households and places of employment.

With an extensive professional career in Information Technology and Project Management, Los managed and led one fourth of Dell Inc's global IT portfolios for over two years from Dell's C.I.O office and headquarters in Round Rock, Texas. He works with the State of Texas and the US Federal Government based in Austin Texas governing its Information Technology interests.

In his spare time Los travels the country as a personal brand and motivational speaker to scores of businesses, colleges and universities. Los' ability to deliver powerful motivational and economical performances has propelled him to the top of many local and regional speakers' lists in Texas and Oklahoma. Los delivers an inspirational message coupled with current and coveted knowledge of the business world, which rivals the best resources published and recorded. He is a valuable resource for anyone interested in surviving and winning in the business world today.

My readers and audiences have seen that I work hard to practice what I teach. No matter who reads this book or hears me speak; my goal is always to provide you something you will find valuable and powerful in your own life.

Much Success – Los Ellis

• • • •

PUT YOUR BEST SHARPIE FORWARD

Use a black Sharpie marker to give your favorite business shoe soles a lasting buff and shine

Unwanted scuffs and marks can appear on the soles of our dress shoes just as we are trying to make a valued impression in route to an important interview or meeting. Scuffs to your shoes can send a negative message about your attention to detail and personal brand to others.

A permanent "black" Sharpie's ink will match most business and dress shoe soles sold today and provide a lasting shine. Conventional shoe polish may not be readily available at the office, but a black Sharpie is a common item in most business and office buildings.

Conventional shoe polish can provide a desired lasting shine to complement your shoe's recently Sharpie buffed shoe sole appearance.

● ● ● ●

ASK FOR A REFERENCE – GET THE JOB

Ask people in your network if you may call on them for a personal or professional <u>Reference</u>

People in your networks are 30% more likely to recommend and promote your resume for prospective employment opportunities when they have committed to providing a reference.

Their commitment indirectly says "I believe in your ability be a solid professional and I am willing to put my reputation on the line for you".

This means when you ask someone if you may use them as a reference, they may also actually FIND your next job for you.

Be certain to thank your contributors for their future reference and any feedback you receive.

● ● ● ●

TELL "ME" ABOUT YOURSELF

This question is actually an ice breaker for you to let business leaders know about your abilities, not just about your identity.

Tell them your full name

Talk briefly about your education

Talk about a project you lead or worked on

Emphasize experiences and skills which makes you relevant for the Job

Don't mention those well-known taboo subjects like:

Salary

Age

Bad Habits

Political Affiliations

● ● ● ●

LEARN A PERSON'S NAME

If you cannot pronounce a colleague or interviewer's name call his/her voice mail after working hours

Here is an opportunity to receive immediate brownie points with a new colleague or interviewer.

Most people will state their name in their mailbox greeting. Many times the person will pronounce their name as they like it to be pronounced by others. They will definitely appreciate you for going the extra effort to learning the correct pronunciation of their name.

Bonus: Insert your colleague's name in *Google Images* to help determine gender and become familiar with their face prior to meeting with him/her for the first time.

● ● ● ●

PURCHASE SHOES

½

SIZE LARGER

Invest in cushioned "heel inserts" for each pair of shoes you own

Research studies reveal, taller people earn more income and are provided additional leadership opportunities. A set of cushioned heel inserts can add up to a ½ or full inch to your standing height making you appear taller.

Heel inserts can help increase your standing posture, soften your walk and add up to a full inch to your overall height.

Bonus: An increase in height also supports improvements of self-esteem and confidence.

● ● ● ●

STANDING IS A LEADER'S PODIUM

Standing when you talk will get you noticed faster and command viewer's attention

Standing, when speaking, has been the preferred method to grab the attention of others by leaders. Throughout history and still today, educators, business persons and politicians use this timeless command of attention.

The fastest way to get noticed in a room filled with people is to yell out a response or question. However if you want to be noticed without appearing out of line; try standing tall when you are speaking. People looking at you will subconsciously view you as a person with something meaningful and necessary to share.

Imagine you are required to stand at a podium each time you begin to speak. This technique will help ensure you command attention and display good posture to everyone with whom you communicate.

● ● ● ●

MENTOR ABOVE THE LINE

Identify multiple mentors to assist you in achieving your goals

To maximize your opportunities for success many successful people recommend having multiple mentors. Having a personal and professional mentor is a minimum requirement for success. It is up to you to identify who is best to fulfill you mentorship.

To help identify the best mentor, I have suggested two types of mentors to help begin your search.

Mentor #1: "Personal" or "Life Coach" mentors – This person will help you optimize opportunities in your personal life.

Example: Family Member or Community Leader

Mentor #2: "Skip Level" mentors – While your current manager is a natural first choice, I would not recommend it. I recommend identifying a mentor at least one level above your current manager or someone in a different work area than you are currently working.

> This will increase your chances of support and growth. The selection of someone other than your direct manager may also increase your opportunities for a promotion. Having a "Skip Level" mentor increases the possibilities of your mentor helping to promote you to the next level…. just under their command!

Be certain to regularly thank your mentor for their efforts and the support they provide you, regularly. He or she is making a valuable investment and an important contribution to your development.

● ● ● ●

DRESS FOR THE JOB ON FRIDAYS

Always dress one step above the status quo on Casual Fridays

You know the saying; "You can't judge a book by its cover"? Well that only applies to books and not your work environment. What you wear at the office speaks volumes about you to your co-workers and management teams.

Show off the best YOU to your co-workers and management teams on Casual Friday's by dressing a step above the Casual Friday employee. Let them know you take your job serious and you come prepared (dressed for work) to assist customers and co-workers every day, even on Casual Fridays.

Dressing for the job you want will alert others that you are always prepared to lead and look the part of a serious leader.

• • • •

BE KNOWN AS A RESOURCE PEOPLE CAN COUNT ON

People will call on you as a valued resource for suggestions, ideas and future connections.

Each one of us possesses a set of skills or trade we do well. It is your responsibility to market and display those skills and trade as a resource that provides value to others.

When you provide a clear understanding of your skills and expertise others will look to you as a resource they can count on when the need arises. You will begin increasing your visibility to customers and business ventures (on-line and in person).

You can display your skills, trades and expertise through many mediums and devices like: Social media, local advertisement and old fashion, word of mouth. I suggest a combination of all three to clearly communicate with a wide variety of people and businesses.

• • • •

YOUR PHYSICAL APPEARANCE DOES MATTER

Research suggests most hiring decisions are made within the first 60 - 90 seconds of an interview

Human Resource experts agree, interviewers may not offer advice on your appearance, but this does not mean they are not grading you on it. Your appearance will count more than the substance of your interview in most situations because most interviewers may have already formed an opinion of you within the first 60 seconds of meeting you and viewing your appearance.

It is always worth asking a friend, family member or co-worker to review your appearance one final time before you walk into your next interview.

Arrive to your next interview with a nice dark colored suit, neatly pressed shirt, groomed nails and hair, moisturized skin and don't forget; a fresh breath!

• • • •

SHAKE HANDS ON TOP

Try to shake hands with yours on top. This displays leadership and dominance

Handshakes are synonymous with meeting new people, greeting old friends and completing business ventures. But handshakes are also synonymous with leadership and dominance.

To display dominance and control in your handshake you should always try to be to the right of the handshake. This positioning will ensure your hand is always on the top of the handshake making you appear to be more dominant and in control.

Try to be the first to release the handshake to establish control of the ensuing conversation and meeting.

● ● ● ●

FLY IN STYLE – FIRST CLASS

Join your favorite frequent flier program and take the challenge

Call your preferred airline and ask to join their elite member's challenge before your next series of flights

Example: You can join American Airlines "Gold Challenge" by calling (800-433-7300) their elite members program to request their "Gold Challenge". This challenge may require a one-time nominal fee.

Take scheduled flights as usual with the airline to receive your elite status early by traveling just 25% of the required "Gold" or "Platinum" miles required within a three month period.

Once completed you will receive all of the privileges of an elite traveler:

Travel in first class whenever empty seats are available.

Upgrade any purchased ticket to first class for as little - as a $30 online fee.

NO 1st or 2nd baggage fees on checked baggage.

Express boarding and screening regardless of ticket type or seat purchased.

● ● ● ●

Collection 2 - Life Keys

I have found that the hidden keys to a better life are found in the hearts and giving of oneself to others. Helping others must be a coupled vessel of generosity that delivers consistently and whole heartedly.

A friend of mine and best-selling author, Stephen Paul West, wrote a biography about me. He pointed out that he noticed I was actively involved in the lives of many people. He stated that "Each of us is more than our reflection in the mirror and a well written biography is only one dimension to who we really are". The biography was derived directly from previous literature he had read, but I hope it creates a sense of validity in your own hearts.

• • • •

Los Ellis resides in sunny Austin TX where he is a mentor, uncle and adoptive parent to his nephew Kendrick Ellis. Los' commitment to personal and community development is a testament to his devotion of education and community upliftment.

His charitable and volunteer base extends from his commitment as a lead team member of the Texas "Mobile Loaves and Fishes" team which provides meals, clothing and living supplies to the Texas homeless and under-serviced population since 2005.

He also serves as a sign language interpreter for many of Austin's homeless residents and citizens. Los also volunteered with the Livestrong Foundation where he donated his time to help survivors of cancer.

In his spare time, Los travels the country as a personal brand coach and motivational speaker to many business professionals, universities and organizations. Los' ability to deliver powerful motivational and economical performances has propelled him to the top of many local and regional business and university's speakers' lists in Texas, Oklahoma and California. Los delivers an inspirational message coupled with current

> and coveted knowledge of the business world, which rivals the best resources published and recorded. He is a valuable resource for anyone interested in surviving and winning in the business world today.

● ● ● ●

The theme, as Stephen Paul, pointed out, was that I actually live the motivational community and educational practices that I teach. I find this to be an important part of who I am, what I stand for and building confidence within my readers and audience (and the fact a colleague made me promise to say all this *smile*).

● ● ● ●

Life occasionally delivers us a series of endless winding roads. At some time or another, we all imagine what it would be like to have the perfect life. We all daydream of wealth, job-satisfaction and of things that we believe would make us totally happy.

Life doesn't always provide us with a net basket of things. In fact, a great deal of life is spent dealing with our separation from things and connecting with people. But this is all right, because THINGS cannot grant us a magical happy life. It certainly helps to have money and fancy gadgets, but my goal is for you to be happy and empowered without becoming a servant to the things we can buy.

This chapter is dedicated to those "Hidden Keys" that will empower you to reinvest in a full and vibrant life.

• • • •

BUILD MEANINGFUL NETWORKS

Introduce yourself to three (3) new people a week

People like to do business with people they know. Consistently introducing yourself to new people helps to keep your network full and regenerative. Your network is the most important tool in your development portfolio.

Most networking experts will tell you, "People like people who take an interest in people".

Networking is an inexpensive way to market you. When people know who you are they are more likely to engage in business with you. People will refer you to business and personal connections if they know, like and trust you.

● ● ● ●

DO NOT ASK FOR DONATIONS

Don't ask people for donations, instead ask people to invest in your cause or event.

People will invest in you and your causes before they donate to them because many people view investments as a promise to return something of value for their investment.

Donations are recognized as a one-time giving with no expectation of a return for donations.

When people investment in you they are making a commitment to help you succeed with the expectation that you will be successful in return.

● ● ● ●

TURN WRIST WATCH FACING INSIDE – PUT YOUR CELL PHONE FACEDOWN

If you put people on a clock when they talk to you, then you devalue them.

If you turn your watch facing inside it is a corporate sign of respect during meetings. Management will be amazed that you know this timeless little secret and it may score you a few points with management.

If you check your cell phone while engaged in a conversation or meeting you may give the impression that you are not fully engaged. Show your dedication to the topic at hand by turning your cell phones on silent or facedown to avoid the temptation to use it.

Bonus: When your wrist watch is facing inside, you can respectfully monitor the time you have remaining to complete your presentation or correspondence with a colleague.

• • • •

WRITE ON YOUR FURNITURE

Use multi-colored dry erase markers to write on your mirrors and computer monitors

Studies show the average person spends forty-five minutes a day staring into our restroom mirror while preparing for the day's events. That's more than five hours of time to visualize your goals each week.

Research confirms we achieve personal goals three times faster and with greater satisfaction when we write them down and view them regularly

That is why I recommend you write your accomplishments, goals, reminders, key dates and other important things you want to remember or achieve on your restroom mirror with a dry erase marker.   .

Dry erase markers wipe 'clean' from mirrors and computer monitors with any dry tissue or napkin paper so update your goals and accomplishments regularly.

● ● ● ●

KEEP YOUR GLASS HALF FULL

At conferences and dinners keep your glass half full. Don't top it off right away.

If you do not have an interest in a conversation with an individual or group or find you need to leave for other reasons, you can excuse yourself to refresh your drink. This is respectful exit strategy that preserves and respects the feelings of others.

This can method can also be used as a way to gain the interest of someone you would like talk to without an audience present. Asking someone to join you to refresh your half-filled drinks provides an opportunity for you to deliver your rehearsed "elevator speech".

● ● ● ●

WATCH YOUR LIPS

Many people can read lip movement from a distance.

Your lips may be conveying a message totally different than the actual words coming from your mouth. As a volunteer sign-language interpreter and lip reader, I am more aware about the impact of lip reading and the potential to see something which differs from what is actually spoken.

People, who are not trained in lip reading, may still be able to read your lips. So be careful to clearly convey the message you want others to receive.

Try this example:

Silently mouth the word "Colorful" to a friend standing at least a foot away from you. Then ask them if they understood what you said to them from a distance. They will assume you said "I love you" and not "Colorful".

After you conduct this test, email your results to me at: info@losellis.com

● ● ● ●

A Bonus Key - A Teachable Heart

Collection 3 - Bonus Material on University and Life-long Learning

This book has lots of white space in the margins. The layout is designed for a reader to write their own thoughts and ideas in the margins. It is a wide-open document for YOUR continued personal growth.

The greater concept taught within "The Hidden Keys To Life and Business Success" is being a 'teachable heart' your entire life. Many of my prepared keynote presentations are directly tailored for companies, universities and local independent school districts. Even without going to 'college' a person who is teachable is a person who can be successful.

I am a graduate of the University of Oklahoma's Michael F. Price - College of Business, where I was one of the five founders and creators of the Sooner Information Network, the University of Oklahoma's first student web portal and information center. I also served as the College of Business student leadership president and remains a life member of the esteemed business fraternity, *Delta Sigma Pi,* where I served as one of five elected Provincial Vice Presidents and sat on the National Board of Directors for 2009- 2012, helping to shape, direct and enhance the goals, and leadership direction of the organization. have been presented with multiple honoraria and awards for my creative and energizing contributions to education along with multiple certifications from accredited universities around the country.

● ● ● ●

You can see from my biography that educational and business empowerment is a key to my lifelong development and goals. I am drawn to the endless opportunities within education and business. My collections of "Hidden Keys" are designed to motivate my fellow educators and business persons in their adventures of learning something new every day.

● ● ● ●

BUILD A SURVIVAL KIT FOR SUCCESS

Carry your resumes with you (always) in expectation of the job you want.

In a time when employment opportunities come and go rapidly, it is important to keep your skills current and well documented within one or two resumes.

Be prepared to share your resume with employers, mentors and references in multiple formats and mediums. I recommend keeping five hard paper copies and two digital (thumb drive or compact disc) copies on hand at all times. Store copies of your resume in the trunk of your automobile or carry bags.

You may want to invest in a nice folder leather binder to secure your most recent resumes and cover letters. Remember appearances still matters.

● ● ● ●

ACT LIKE A CHIPMUNK

Gather as much information as you can handle.

Chipmunks understand the value of gathering resources and storing it in a safe place until a time when its value is irreplaceable and required in the future. Information gathering and storage is an important resource and asset to businesses and our personal successes. The more information you have access to, the more valuable you are to others.

To gain additional opportunities to gather resources, you can volunteer to work on a new project on a non-traditional holiday to stay ahead of others and learn new information to enhance your value.

● ● ● ●

TIME YOUR REQUESTS

People are most persuadable after thanking someone.

Try timing your requests by asking someone for help on a project immediately after you've been thanked by them. This is the best time to request their support on a special project or business venture.

People are also most persuasive after being thanked because they feel a sense of accomplishment and success for doing something appreciated by others.

• • • •

MARKET AND SELL YOUR BRAND

Join a social network for personal and professional profile

You will need to create two social networking profiles. Your first networking profile should represent your personal/social side. Share your (first) personal/social profile with friends and family.

Share items like; Photos and videos of your family vacations, graduations and everyday tasteful activities

I also recommend that you create a second social networking profile to market and sell your professional profile and brand. Your professional profile should be a profile you can openly share with potential employers and co-workers.

Share items like; Professional looking photos and videos of yourself, updates of your attendance at conferences and educational events, resumes, cover letters, professional blogs, work history, awards, degrees and certifications.

Both, your personal and professional profiles comprise of your Brand. Using online social networking site can help support building your brand.

● ● ● ●

SERVE A PRAISE SANDWICH

Begin discussions, meetings and difficult conversations with positive feedback.

Productive discussions and conversations consist of thoughtful statements and a planned desired outcome. Discussions and conversations should also be polite and responsible when delivering negative feedback or a request to address a development opportunity.

One of the best methods professionals use to champion challenging or difficult conversations is a "Praise Sandwich".

A Praise Sandwich consists of:

- An opening statement of praise about the individual or their work.
- Addressing any development opportunities (items you would like to see changed) quickly.
- Closing the meeting with another praise of the individual or their work.

The recipient of your praise sandwich will feel encouraged to work towards the changes you addressed!

• • • •

End

AUTHORS CONTACT INFORMATION

Los Ellis is an Austin Texas Keynote Speaker and Novelist.

Los is also a frequent Keynote Speaker on topics including:

Bullying in "Your" Workplace

What is Workplace Bullying? Reclaiming Your Professional Dignity from Aggressive Bullies.

Who Values Your Personal Brand

Developing a Personal That Promotes and Enhance Your Professional Career.

3 Key Reasons Businesses Fail

Effective Methods to Avoid Common Mistakes Entrepreneurs Encounter Leading to Business Failure.

Negotiating a Salary Package

How Much Am I Worth; and How Do I Convince Others of My Net Value?

Your Body Language Is Talking About You

Learn Nine Proven Techniques to Manage Your

Body Language at Work and In Your Personal Relationships.

To learn more about *Los Ellis*' seminars, publications and keynote performances

Email : Info@losellis.com

Website: www.losellis.com

Phone: (507) 5LOS-ISM or (507) 556-7476

Additional Contact Information

Website: www.losellis.com

Blog Spot: http://4minutes-withlosellis.blogspot.com

Expert File: http://expertfile.com/experts/los.ellis

Twitter: https://twitter.com/losellis

Facebook: http://www.facebook.com/losellis

Made in the USA
Lexington, KY
24 March 2014